I08804821

IMAGES
of America

SOUTHERN CALIFORNIA ROAD RACING

The scene is Laguna Seca Raceway, located in the coastal foothills near Monterey, California, as a Lotus 7 sports car kicks up a cloud of dust while spectators stand casually by the side of the track during a race on a hot day in 1964. (Courtesy of John Masterson.)

On the Cover: Bob Oker, driving an AC Bristol, passes the camera at Paramount Ranch race track in 1957. Note the Western movie set in the background. (Courtesy of Bill Haislett.)

IMAGES
of America

SOUTHERN CALIFORNIA ROAD RACING

Tony Baker

ARCADIA
PUBLISHING

ISBN 978-1-4671-0362-6

Published by Arcadia Publishing
Charleston, South Carolina

Printed in the United States of America

Library of Congress Control Number: 2019936761

For all general information, please contact Arcadia Publishing:
Telephone 843-853-2070
Fax 843-853-0044
E-mail sales@arcadiapublishing.com
For customer service and orders:
Toll-Free 1-888-313-2665

Visit us on the Internet at www.arcadiapublishing.com

Dedicated to John "Bat" Masterson.

Contents

ACKNOWLEDGMENTS

I want to express my thanks to the many people who helped me put this book together. First, thanks to David Steele at the American Hot Rod Foundation who provided encouragement and many valuable contacts. Special thanks go to Virginia-based motorsports historian Joel Driskill, for providing the images and facts for the first chapter; former California Sports Car Club flagman Bill Haislett, for images and racing lore; Judy and Jeff Masterson, for the use of the late John Masterson's images and research materials; Joe Danely, for images and helping to get the project started, and Lee Hammock and Barry Atsatt, for images and research material. Thanks go to my photo technician Gil Trevino. And, of course, thanks to my son Thomas, my old buddy Harry Mishkin, and Adam, Tiffanie, Josh, and the rest of the gang at Squashed Grapes Winery and Jazz Bar.

INTRODUCTION

Road racing is largely overlooked today in the annals of California's motorsports history. The immense success of drag racing in the 1960s stole a lot of the limelight. But from the early 1950s to the mid-1960s, the sport flared brightly, attracting tens of thousands of people to race events. Road racing had everything—action, danger, exotic cars, star drivers—all taking place among the beautiful scenery of Southern California.

The road racing scene in California began in the postwar era of the late 1940s. Like drag racing, which began about the same time, it was made up largely of amateur enthusiasts, and the sport gradually went from amateur to semi-professional and eventually wound up as a million-dollar enterprise where the amateur enthusiasts were crowded out by big operators and large corporations.

Car culture in Southern California exploded after the war, and Los Angeles was the epicenter. Hot rodding and drag racing were all the rage with teenagers and those in their early 20s, and there was a slightly older group who preferred a different kind of driving. Made up of people from many different walks of life, quite a few had been exposed to European-built sports cars during their war service and noticed the difference in performance and handling from domestic cars. While American cars were undoubtedly powerful and well suited for the American highway, they lacked the nimbleness that European sports models possessed. Many of the roads in Southern California wind through coastal and desert foothills, and driving a small car with good handling and quick acceleration on them was an exhilarating experience that is taken for granted today. But driving the average late 1940s American sedan, with its heavy body roll and poor brakes, on such roads could be a nerve-wracking experience for most drivers. When sports cars like the British-built MG-TC appeared on the scene in California, they were a revelation to many enthusiasts who quickly noticed how well the cars performed on roads like Mulholland Drive in Los Angeles and Highway 150 in Ventura, and how much fun, or "sporty," this type of driving could be.

As enthusiasts will do, they began forming clubs and organizations, with the California Sports Car Club (also known as "Cal Club" and CSCC) and the Sports Car Club of America (SCCA) being the biggest, with a wide variety of smaller local and special interest clubs as well. The clubs began to organize races within themselves and with other clubs for that most basic objective in racing, to see who was the fastest. The members of these clubs, as mentioned before, came from many different walks of life.

There were the amateur hobbyist drivers, usually professional men like doctors, lawyers, and small businessmen, who loved to race and had the spare money for what could be a very expensive hobby. Garage and body shop owners like Max Balchowsky and Chuck Porter, who built their own very competitive "specials," and a legion of small-time operators whose cars were made on a shoestring at home in the garage. Several enthusiasts were also car dealers or sold foreign car parts. There were women drivers like Ruth Levy, Ann Meyers, and Ginny Sims. Hollywood movie stars like James Dean, Steve McQueen, and James Garner were drawn to the sport too. And then there were the millionaire entrepreneur/industrialist sportsmen like Lance Reventlow, Briggs Cunningham, and Sterling Edwards, all of whom decided to manufacture their own marques. Finally, there were the serious drivers. Men like Phil Hill, Ken Miles, Dan Gurney, and others who seemed a class apart from the rest.

The first few races featuring European sports cars were held at the now-defunct Carrell Speedway, a half-mile dirt oval track that was located on South Vermont Avenue in Los Angeles, but this was not really the right venue. A proper road-racing course should possess a variety of curves, straights, and changes in elevation. Successful races were held on temporary courses laid out at Torrey Pines near San Diego and Pebble Beach on the Monterey Peninsula. Santa Barbara Airport at Goleta and the parking lot of the Los Angeles County Fairgrounds at Pomona were the sites of many popular road races over the years. In a short time, purpose-built race tracks or "speedways" began to appear. Some, like Willow Springs, remain today as well-designed, challenging, and safe courses. Others, like Riverside and Paramount Ranch, could be quite unforgiving, and fatalities during a race led to the closure of more than one track.

Early races were mostly club affairs with fairly limited attendance. The first meets at Pebble Beach had a decidedly upper-crust feel to them. Popular interest increased as the 1950s progressed, however, and by 1960, crowd sizes averaged over 30,000 per race at events like Pomona and Santa Barbara. There were two competing bi-weekly newspapers reporting on the racing news in the region featuring the drivers and other colorful personalities of the day—and there were colorful personalities. There were drivers like the quiet, introspective Phil Hill, the greatest American formula driver in history, and the mercurial Englishman Ken Miles, seemingly unbeatable until his death testing the experimental Ford J Car at Riverside in 1966. There were dealers like John Von Nuemann, who owned the legendary Competition Motors on Vine Street in Hollywood. Von Nuemann was instrumental in establishing Porsche, and later Ferrari, as luxury sport marques on the West Coast. Actor James Dean purchased the Porsche 550 Spyder that he was killed in from Competition Motors, and it was the dealership's chief mechanic, Rolf Wuthertich, riding in the car with Dean at the time of the accident.

Road racing was certainly dangerous. Besides Dean's accident in 1955, the fatal crash of popular driver Ernie McAfee in a race at Pebble Beach a year later ended that location's use as a venue, although it was replaced a few years later by the vastly superior course at nearby Laguna Seca. Two fatalities and a particularly gruesome injury in one day during a race at Paramount Ranch finished racing there forever. Riverside International Raceway was considered a dangerous track and claimed several lives, although a later redesign improved things a bit. Increasing speeds and a series of high-profile accidents throughout the early and mid-1960s led to a reputation for danger that affected all of motorsports. More and more stringent safety regulations and better technology resulted in more highly advanced race cars but also wound up putting the amateur out of business as the cost of building a race-worthy car began to skyrocket.

These factors, plus the cultural and other changes of the late 1960s and early 1970s, led to a slow but steady thinning out of crowd sizes in the region until big tracks like Riverside and Ontario were no longer financially viable and closed, becoming more valuable as real estate developments.

Most of the tracks are gone now, along with the cars and their drivers. Fortunately, the memories remain in the form of stories and photographs.

One

Early Days

In the early 1950s, clubs like the Foreign Car Club of America and the Sports Car Club of America were formed by owners and dealers of the growing stream of European cars that were being imported into the United States. Locally, the California Sports Car Club was founded and came to dominate much of the racing and club action in conjunction with smaller groups like the Long Beach MG Club. The members came from all walks of life and could be movie people, garage mechanics, recent college grads, or young professionals like doctors and lawyers. Seen in this shot of an early club meet, possibly taken at Griffith Park in Los Angeles, are several MGs, a Jaguar XII, and an Austin A40. (Courtesy of Joel Driskill.)

Most Americans first became acquainted with foreign-made sports cars through the British-made MG series, built by Morris Motors, seen here at center. The small, simple MG-TC and MG-TD's sporty handling made them very popular with postwar driving enthusiasts. Another product of Morris, called the Minor, can be seen at far right. (Courtesy of Joel Driskill.)

German cars also began appearing on American shores in the early 1950s. Fast, well-engineered, and expensive, the Porsche 356 was an instant hit on the West Coast. This very early model, identifiable by the slightly kinked windshield, makes its way past onlookers during a club meet. (Courtesy of Joel Driskill.)

These two images, taken at an impromptu club meet held in a shopping center parking lot in the San Fernando Valley, show several MG-TDs flanking a lone Austin A40 Somerset. These meets were a way for owners to get together and tell war stories, share sources for scarce and hard-to-find spare parts, and generally discuss the merits and pitfalls of foreign car ownership. It also exposed the general public to the lifestyle. Early morning get-togethers like this one, held by clubs on weekends in parking lots throughout the state, are still a part of the California car scene. (Both, courtesy of Joel Driskill.)

The earliest races were held on temporary tracks, like the one laid out on some vacant land located in the Torrey Pines State Reserve near San Diego, California. In this image from 1952, a young Phil Hill approaches the camera in Charles Hornburg's Jaguar C type. (Courtesy of Joel Driskill.)

Formerly an Army training base called Camp Callan, the course at Torrey Pines was laid out in part by Cal Club co-founder John Von Nuemann, who was stationed there briefly during the war. In this shot, an Olds-powered Allard J2X is being chased by actor Keenan Wynn's Cadillac-engine Alfa Romeo 8C, driven by Tom Banford. (Courtesy of Joel Driskill.)

Well planned and in a scenic location, the racetrack was situated next to Torrey Pines State Beach. With a variety of turns and straights, it was considered by drivers to be a world-class road racing course. Here, John Fox in his Ferrari 185S is leading a Porsche down the straight. (Courtesy of Joel Driskill.)

After only a few years, the State of California, which owned the land the track was on, decided that the former Army camp would better serve the public as a golf course (which it still is today), and racing was curtailed. In this shot, Irv Robbins in his Cunningham C2R battles it out with an unidentified MG-TC. (Courtesy of Joel Driskill.)

Postwar California was filled with disused airfields of all sizes and descriptions, and they were favorite venues for all types of motorsports. In 1954, road races were held at an active airbase, March Air Force Base (AFB), located in Riverside County. Pictured here is Phil Walters driving a Cunningham C5R. (Courtesy of Joel Driskill.)

An OSCA MT-4 driven by James Simpson passes the camera at March AFB. Originally known as March Field, the base had long been home to heavy bomber squadrons, and at the time this photograph was taken, was being operated by the Cold War–era Strategic Air Command (SAC). (Courtesy of Joel Driskill.)

Ken Miles, at right, passes a group of SAC B-47 bombers and KC-97 air tankers in the first of his two homemade MG specials. Miles would go on to greater fame driving Porsches for John Von Nuemann, and later as a driver for Carroll Shelby and Ford. (Courtesy of Joel Driskill.)

Phil Hill muscles one of the big Cunningham C2-R race cars around the bend at Palm Springs in 1951. The C2-R was the brainchild of millionaire Briggs Cunningham, who built it as one of 27 homologation models for qualification in the 24 hours of Le Mans race. Cunningham never won at Le Mans with the car, but did come close several times. (Courtesy of Joel Driskill.)

Irving Robbins rounds the same corner in a black Cunningham C3. The C3 was the most numerous of the series, equipped as a luxury sports car and powered by a 220-horsepower Chrysler V8. The cars were manufactured at Cunningham's facility in West Palm Beach, Florida. (Courtesy of Joel Driskill.)

This is Bruce Mooney driving a Jowette Jupiter at Palm Springs in 1952. Jowette Cars Ltd., located in the United Kingdom, made its own four-cylinder, horizontally-opposed 1,486-cc engine and had won its class in the 1950 Le Mans race. The cars were said to have poor build quality, and the marque was out of business by 1954. (Courtesy of Joel Driskill.)

New York State race driver Wilbur Lamoreaux was at Palm Springs in his Singer SM and is seen here dicing with Tracy Bird in his MG-TD. Singer, a small British car manufacturer, produced the well-built sports car as a competitor to the MG-T series. (Courtesy of Joel Driskill.)

An unidentified Jaguar XK-120 passes the camera while being chased by Gary Laughlin in his modified Allard J-2X. Laughlin powered his Allard with an Oldsmobile 303-ci V8 and modified the bodywork up front. What appears to be John Edgar's MG special can be seen bringing up the rear. (Courtesy of Joel Driskill.)

Many of the competitors in the 1953 Palm Springs race would go on to be major figures in the road racing scene over the next two decades. Here, Jack McAfee heads toward the camera in a Ferrari 340 America. Jack and his brother Eric (who would be killed racing at Pebble Beach in 1955) were popular and successful drivers. (Courtesy of Joel Driskill.)

Los Angeles–based hot-rodder Bill Stroppe in his flathead Ford–powered Kurtis 500S rounds the turn at an almost identical angle. Barely visible behind him is a very rare Nardi-Danese driven by Bill Kerrigan and powered by a GMC 270-ci straight-six truck engine. (Courtesy of Joel Driskill.)

Even rarer than a Nardi was the Veritas Comet S, pictured here at Palm Springs in 1953 driven by John Beihl. Built in West Germany largely out of BMW 326 parts, the Comet S was powered by a 1,988-cc Heinkel six-cylinder engine. (Courtesy of Joel Driskill.)

John Von Neumann, in the Le Mans Porsche 356 coupe, leads the pack at Palm Springs. Included in this shot are an unidentified Porsche 356 Spyder, Wilbur Lamoraeux in his Singer, and an unidentified MG-TD. (Courtesy of Joel Driskill.)

In this image, a crowd at left gathers around the Cunningham C2R that Phil Hill drove during the race. To the right is Bill David's MG special. The simple design of the MG-T series was easily adaptable to any number of modifications, from installing V8 engines to the addition of special bodies, like this beautiful example by Hagemann Coachbuilders. (Courtesy of Joel Driskill.)

A Jaguar XK-120 driven by Gerry Felnagle is seen here at Palm Springs. Probably the prettiest sports car of the era, the XK was moderately priced compared to similar sports cars on the market. The six-cylinder XK engine produced 150 horsepower at 5,000 rpm. (Courtesy of Joel Driskill.)

Ernie McAfee gets into a bit of trouble on the track at Palm Springs in his XK-120 coupe. Besides the coupe and roadster models, the XK-120 was also available as a convertible, or drop head, coupe. Note the track officials seated on the truck-mounted scaffolding in the background. (Courtesy of Joel Driskill.)

Fiberglass car body pioneer and sports-car builder Bill Devin of Los Angeles owned this Ferrari 212 Export, seen at Palm Springs. That is either Devin himself or Ernie McAfee behind the wheel. A follow-on to Ferrari's successful type 166, the Ghia-bodied 212 was powered by a 2,562-cc engine that produced up to 170 horsepower. (Courtesy of Joel Driskill.)

Vintage-car races were often used to entertain crowds on race days. Here, a group of Brass Era cars from the early 20th century grind their way around the track at Palm Springs in 1953. Public interest in antique or pre–Great Depression–era cars began in the late 1940s and carried on into the 1950s with the formation of clubs like the Antique Automobile Club of America and the Model T Owners Club, both of which are still active. Car No. 6 below appears to be a Ford Model T special. (Both, courtesy of Joel Driskill.)

This new Volkswagen Beetle was entered in the Palm Springs race by the mysteriously named club "Ecurie Von Smitty," which was possibly a cover for Hollywood-based Volkswagen dealer Bob Smith. Beetles were not taken seriously by car buffs when they first came out, but this one apparently gave a good performance, giving more than one MG a lot of trouble. (Courtesy of Joel Driskill.)

A perimeter road on the former Marine Air Station at Goleta just north of Santa Barbara had been the site of drag racing since the late 1940s. By 1953, the CSCC began holding road races there as well. Here, an early Kurtis 500 passes the camera. (Courtesy of Lee Hammock.)

Big Jack McAfee barrels around the turn in a Touring-bodied Ferrari 340 America, closely followed by Bill Stroppe in a Kurtis 500S. The first of the Ferrari America series, the 340 was a big, powerful car designed to be driven long distances. Powered by a Lampredi 4.1-liter twin overhead cam V12 Formula One engine producing 220 horsepower, 23 of the 340 Americas were produced in either Barchetta (roadster) or Berlinetta (sports coupe) models with bodies by Touring, Vignale, Ghia, and Michelotti. The 340, which was built between 1950 and 1952, was replaced by the even larger 342 and 375 models. (Courtesy of Joel Driskill.)

Two

The People

The people involved in road racing came from all walks of life. Most were older by a few years than the hot rod crowd. Because the pursuit was expensive, several were also business owners of one type or another. There were Hollywood movie stars, millionaires, garage owners, and home mechanics who worked regular day jobs, as well as quite a few transplanted Europeans, like Ken Miles (center right), who is seen engaging in heated discussion with Cal Club official and starter Cy Yedor (far left) over his disqualification during the June 1957 meet at Paramount Ranch. Meanwhile, a couple in the background—who appear to be members of the press—expertly crash the photograph. (Courtesy of Bill Haislett.)

One of the biggest stars of the racing scene in California was British-born Ken Miles, seen here piloting John Von Neumann's Porsche. A highly skilled driver, Miles was killed at Riverside in 1966 while testing the prototype J-car, which Ford had intended to replace the popular GT-40 series of race cars. (Courtesy of Bill Haislett.)

Ken Miles engineered the installation of a Porsche engine in the Cooper he is seen driving here. Highly competitive, Miles could also be abrasive when rubbed the wrong way. He was well liked and respected by many in the racing world, but his personality gained him a few enemies too. The editors of *Motor Racing*, a popular racing journal of the day, particularly disliked him. (Courtesy of Bill Haislett.)

Flagmen played an important role in ensuring that the race was being run safely. Using flags to signal drivers in the event of road hazards, several were stationed around the track at various locations. Here, a group at Paramount Ranch hold a pre-race briefing. (Courtesy of Bill Haislett.)

Flagmen also watched for rule violations by the drivers and did a bit of mild crowd control, although this one does not seem too interested in the two spectators who have strayed past the fence at center right. The car visible at far left is none other than Duffy Livingstone's No. 184, the "Eliminator," a Model T dirt-track racer that went road racing. (Courtesy of Bill Haislett.)

A group of flagmen gather for a cup of coffee after a long day officiating at Riverside International Motorway. At far right is the "chariot" built by the Long Beach MG Club for dropping off the judges and flagmen at their various stations around the track. Otto Zipper's ubiquitous VW press van can be seen in the left background. (Courtesy of Bill Haislett.)

The October 1958 meet at Riverside attracted some of the greatest names in road racing. In this image, Le Mans champion Sir Sterling Moss confers with track officials. Due to legal technicalities, Moss was unable to compete in the race. He did, however, run a Lotus around the course on practice day. (Courtesy of John Masterson.)

The proximity to Hollywood at the Riverside meet brought out a decidedly glamorous and cosmopolitan crowd. Here, a group of racing types happily pose with "Miss Corvette." The unidentified driver at left is wearing a Team Mexico racing suit. (Courtesy of John Masterson.)

One of the Hollywood crowd attending the race at Riverside was actress Jill St. John. She is seen here regally ignoring the chaos around her as mechanics and hangers-on mill about. Her husband, millionaire Lance Reventlow, manufactured this Scarab race car. (Courtesy of Bill Haislett.)

Ken Miles, in a Porsche RSK, leads Bob Drake in the Cooper Climax. Drake was an accomplished race car driver who also owned the popular Grand Prix restaurant in Hollywood, which served as a gathering place for the local motorsport community. His wife, Mary Davis, was co-owner and a well-accomplished driver herself. (Courtesy of Bill Haislett.)

Actress Jayne Mansfield was apparently a fan of road racing, as she was seen at many events in the late 1950s. Here, she is at Pomona in 1957 with her husband, bodybuilder and actor Mickey Hargitay, as they make their way past a group of paparazzi. (Courtesy of Bill Haislett.)

Bob Oker leans into the turn as he pilots an Aston Martin DB-3S at Pomona. California native Oker was an experienced racer who got his start on motorcycles. After several serious injuries racing two-wheelers, Oker decided that four wheels might be safer and became a very competitive and popular driver. (Courtesy of Bill Haislett.)

Johnny Von Nuemann enters the top of the frame of this image in his pontoon body Ferrari Testarossa. Von Nuemann was an early postwar advocate for the Ferrari marque and was responsible for the growth in sales and prestige of Ferrari on the West Coast during the 1940s, 1950s, and 1960s. (Courtesy of Bill Haislett.)

Journalists, photographers, and race officials crowd around Chuck Daigh (with a shaved head at left) after his win at Riverside in the first US Grand Prix. Daigh drove Scarab No. 5 to first place in an exciting race that saw the No. 3 Scarab, driven by Lance Reventlow, put out of the race after being rear-ended by Johnny Von Neumann in a Porsche. (Courtesy of Bill Haislett.)

A member of Bill Murphy's crew looks back at the camera with an expression that seems to be either disgust or dismay after engaging in conversation with a local police officer. Note the extensive use of louvers on the rear fender of Murphy's Buick Special. (Courtesy of Bill Haislett.)

Myra Buchanan, in the No. 00 OSCA, is neatly framed between a Porsche Spyder at left and an MGTD at right. Myra was one of a small group of women drivers, including Mary Davis and Ruth Levy, who were successful in the male-dominated sport of road racing. (Courtesy of Bill Haislett.)

Jack Nethercutt tries out his new Ferrari 250 TR during a practice day at Santa Barbara. Nethercutt, heir to a family fortune in cosmetics and also an avid automotive enthusiast, would go on to be chairman of one of the most prestigious car museums in California, the Merle Norman Collection. (Courtesy of Bill Haislett.)

Racing great Mickey Thompson tried his hand at road racing, as he did with most other types of motorsports. He is seen here at Pomona in 1957 driving this rare Kurtis 500SX, the first of only six built. Built in Glendale, California, in 1955, this car had a long career in racing and was restored in 2003. (Courtesy of Bill Haislett.)

Arnie Kaine drops the checkered flag before John "Bat" Masterson as he runs his early MGA past the finish line during a production class race at Goleta. Al Torres was the best-known Cal Club flagman, famous for his high jumps while waving drivers in. (Courtesy of John Masterson.)

Bat Masterson (in the driver's seat) was a popular and well-known figure in the Southland racing scene for nearly two decades. Both as a driver and owner, Masterson was an enthusiastic supporter of the sport and also contributed many of the images in this book. (Photograph by James La Tourette.)

This photograph, taken on October 18, 1964, at Laguna Seca, shows Roger Penske (left, with goggles) and Dan Gurney relaxing after the Pacific Grand Prix, in which Penske came in first place driving a Chaparral 2, and Gurney a close second. When this picture was taken, both young drivers were approaching the peak of their careers and would go on to great success both in racing and in business. (Courtesy of John Masterson.)

The image above shows a very young Pedro Rodriguez at the 1956 Riverside seated in his Porsche 550 preparing for a practice run where he impressed all there with his skill. The image below was taken a few years later at Sebring, when Rodriguez tried out Formula Junior racing. The car is an OSCA FJ 1100. Rodriguez would go on to a very successful career in Formula One, driving for the teams of Ferrari, Cooper, Lotus, and BRM. He was killed in 1971 while driving a Ferrari 512M in a race at Nuremberg, West Germany. (Both, courtesy of John Masterson.)

Three

The Tracks

For a long time, racetracks of one kind or another were springing up like mushrooms throughout the Southland. There were the temporary road courses on old military bases, and airports were being used frequently as well. The state fairground at Pomona, California, converted its parking lot into a track for racing events that attracted huge crowds. Soon, race courses, or speedways, designed by top drivers started being carved out of remote locations in the foothills and deserts north of Los Angeles. This shot, taken at the famed desert track Willow Springs, shows the starting lineup for a 1954 race. From left to right are Carl Shipman in an Allard J2X, a Jaguar C-Type driven by J.A. Jackson, and car No. 5, the Troutman-Barnes Special. (Courtesy of Joel Driskill.)

One of the most challenging speedways laid out during the 1950s was Paramount Ranch. Located in the otherworldly beauty of the Santa Monica Mountains, Paramount Ranch was the scene of many famous motion pictures of the 1930s and 1940s. By 1956, Paramount Pictures, the property's original owner, was long gone, and the land was owned by a group of investors who decided to build a road racing course on it. Designed by a pair of experienced drivers, Ken Miles and Dick Van Laanen, the two-mile course featured an over/underpass and several changes of elevation as well as grandstands and a pit area. The roadway was narrow in places, and there were many difficult turns, laying traps for unwary drivers. Racing went on for 18 months until a race in 1957 when two fatalities and a serious injury occurred in one day. (Courtesy of Bill Haislett.)

Sudden rain showers could be a common springtime event in the Santa Monica Mountains. The driver of this open Alpha-Romeo Giulietta Spyder takes a soaking as he comes out of a curve at Paramount Ranch. (Courtesy of Bill Haislett.)

Chuck Daigh in the white Troutman-Barnes Special chases the No. 133 Jaguar D-Type driven by Jerry Austin out of the long straight and into turn one at Paramount Ranch during the June 10 main event in which Daigh took first place and Austin second. (Courtesy of Bill Haislett.)

Bob Oker, driving car dealer Ed Savin's AC Bristol, leans into a turn as he passes the Western town set that abutted the race track, which itself would be used as a movie set. Oker later piloted Ferraris and an Aston Martin DBR2 to some success on the California road-racing circuit. (Courtesy of Bill Haislett.)

Chuck Porter's Mercedes special is seen here bearing a bit of damage on the front left fender as a result of a "nerfing" battle. Nerfing is a term in racing when aggressive driving results in contact between two or more cars, usually around the wheel, fender, and quarter-panel area. Note the variety of imported cars visible in the background. (Courtesy of Bill Haislett.)

Chuck Porter's SLS was featured in the sordid 1957 Paramount racing melodrama *The Devil's Hairpin*, starring Cornel Wilde and Jean Wallace, which was filmed at the ranch. A coat of matte white paint and a change of race number, plus the addition of an egg-crate front grill and fin behind the headrest was enough to alter the SLS's appearance for the movie. Valuable today only for the footage depicting action at Paramount Ranch, the movie itself was a turgid potboiler that received very poor reviews and was quickly taken out of circulation by the studio. Parked next to the SLS above is a DKW Junior. Below, actor Tyrone Power can be seen at center left, kneeling in front of the car and wearing sunglasses. (Both, courtesy of Bill Haislett.)

The rear of Jack Nethercutt's Lotus 9 is seen to good advantage in this shot. Car No. 184, in the right background, is Duffy Livingston's "Eliminator." A Model T hot rod that really had no place among the Coopers and Ferraris in the racing scene, Livingston's Eliminator still raced very competitively for a number of years. (Courtesy of Bill Haislett.)

The rear wheel of Frank Woodward's Alfa Romeo Spyder is just leaving the ground as it rolls into a curve at Paramount Ranch. Woodward, of La Habra, California, has prepared the car for racing by removing the bumpers, hubcaps, and windshield, and taping the headlights as well. (Courtesy of Bill Haislett.)

Instead of driving one of his "Ol Yaller" creations during the March 9, 1957, meet at Paramount Ranch, Max Balchowsky drove this Buick-powered Doretti. Built in England by the Swallow Coachbuilding Company, the sports car originally came with Triumph TR-2 running gear. (Courtesy of Bill Haislett.)

Walter Garlic of Sherman Oaks is seen here driving Frank Millard's red Alfa Spyder Veloce at Paramount Ranch. Of note is Garlic's casual racing attire, consisting of a plaid flannel shirt and a pair of khaki pants. (Courtesy of Bill Haislett.)

Richie Ginther lifts the rear wheel of Joe Lubin's Aston Martin DB-3S on one of the curves at Paramount Ranch. Lubin was the West Coast distributor for Cooper and had a shop on Firestone Boulevard in Los Angeles where he sold used sports and racing cars. (Courtesy of Bill Haislett.)

This British racing green Jaguar D-Type was driven to first place in the over 1,500 cc class main event during the March 9, 1957, meet at Paramount Ranch by Jerry Austin of Arcadia, California. Austin engaged Chuck Daigh, driving the Troutman-Barnes Special, in a cliff-hanging race to the finish line, beating Daigh by one second. (Courtesy of Bill Haislett.)

The black No. 313 MGTD driven by George De Lado swerves around turn five at Paramount Ranch. De Lado, of Hollywood, frequently raced under various pseudonyms like Attila the Hun, Attila G. De Lado, or sometimes just Attila. Car No. 237 is an MG Mk2 driven by Norah Taylor of Arcata, California. (Courtesy of Bill Haislett.)

Popular driver Lou Brero, in his blue Ferrari Monza, is being harried around turn nine at Paramount Ranch by another Ferrari Monza driven by Johnny Von Nuemann. Judging by the damage visible on the Monza's rear fender, contact has already been made with either another car or a guardrail. (Courtesy of Bill Haislett.)

Johnny Von Nuemann comes up on the inside of turn five at Paramount Ranch. The MGTD alongside him carries race No. 124, which was used by Jim Firestone of Monterey Park, California. Since Firestone usually drove a Frazier Nash Le Mans replica, maybe he was trying out an MG that day in a practice run. (Courtesy of Bill Haislett.)

Bob Drake, in Joe Lubin's Cooper Climax, is seen leading Ken Miles in the Von Nuemann Porsche-Cooper down the hill from turn six at Paramount Ranch in a spirited fight for first place. The white Porsche Speedster is being driven by Jimmy Moore of Hollywood, and Louis Thompson of Granada Hills is in the MGTD. (Courtesy of Bill Haislett.)

It is November 17, 1956, and Bob Drake, in the No. 249 Cooper Climax, and Ken Miles, in the No. 50 Porsche-Cooper, are passing slower cars as they round the top of turn six at Paramount Ranch. The orange No. 26 is an MG special driven by Bud Hand of Los Angeles, and the turquoise No. 77 is the MGA driven by E. Forbes "Robbie" Robinson of Glendale. (Courtesy of Bill Haislett.)

Ken Miles in the silver Porsche-Cooper passes George "Attila" De Lado in the black MGTD at Paramount Ranch as the old studio scenery dock building stands in the background. During the ranch's heyday in the 1930s and 1940s, it was the backdrop for many major studio productions. By the 1950s, it was used mainly for B-grade Westerns and television shows. (Courtesy of Bill Haislett.)

Eric Hauser, in Max Balchowsky's "Ol Yeller" (left), and Richie Ginther, in Joe Lubin's Aston Martin DB-3S, head down the long, narrow straight during the beginning of a race at Paramount Ranch. The cloud of dust in the background is about where the start/finish line would be. Coming are turns one and two, which combined to make a dangerous, hard 180-degree right turn. (Courtesy of Bill Haislett.)

A group of officials gather around Jack Nethercutt's Lotus 11 after a slight mishap at Paramount Ranch. While the track was in a beautiful location, it was a very challenging course, even for experienced drivers. Two deaths that occurred during a competition later in the 1957 season ended racing there forever. (Courtesy of Bill Haislett.)

One of the great courses was the temporary speedway laid out using the parking lot and drag strip at the Los Angeles County Fairgrounds in Pomona, California. Over 10 years, starting in 1955, races were held there that attracted huge crowds from the nearby city of Los Angeles. This shot, taken at the July 27, 1957, meet at Pomona shows the big event, which was the race for modifieds over 1,500 cc, getting underway. Eric Hauser in "Ol Yaller I" leads a pack including Johnny Von Nuemann in the Ferrari Testarossa, Chuck Daigh in the Troutman-Barnes Special, and Bob Oker in an Aston Martin. (Courtesy of Bill Haislett.)

The start/finish line at Pomona was partway down the straight at the beginning of the pits, and the straight led into an underpass. Here, a race for production types is about to start. In the background is the Allied Van Lines moving van that served as an impromptu officials' stand. (Courtesy of Bill Haislett.)

The underpass at Pomona was one of the most distinctive features of the course. Drivers would come out from under the bridge and turn left into a difficult set of S-curves that caused many a rollover. Here, a Corvette leads an Austin Healey 100/4. (Courtesy of Bill Haislett.)

As drivers left the underpass, they encountered the troublesome turn two. Coming up a slight rise and turning gently to the left, it was a trap for unaware drivers. Cars on the outside, like the Jaguar XK-120 at center above, tended to fishtail into the hay bales at right. Cars on the tightly packed inside had it worse. Below, what looks like an AC Bristol has lost it and is taking a Mercedes along for the ride, while a Corvette is about to join in. The situation got so bad that course marshal Alan Moss had a penalty levied against any driver who spun out on this particular curve. (Both, courtesy of Bill Haislett.)

Turn six at Pomona was a horseshoe curve that led into the short straight before turn seven. Here, a group of production-class cars, including four MGs, go around the bend. The temporary nature of the converted parking lot/race track is apparent. (Courtesy of Bill Haislett.)

The Mercedes Owners Club gathers together in a far corner of the lot during a break in racing at Pomona. Three 300 SLs can be seen, as well as Chuck Porter's SLS. At far left is an Austin Healey 100/4, and to the right, a photographer shoots a Duesenberg. (Courtesy of Bill Haislett.)

Racing has come to a halt at Pomona as the drivers pitch in with flagmen and track officials to clean up the mess after a car took out several hay bales. Note the crowd of spectators on the hill in the background overlooking the parking lot race course. (Courtesy of Bill Haislett.)

Chuck Daigh runs the Troutman-Barnes Special down the back straight at Pomona. The first creation of the team of Dick Troutman and Don Barnes, who would later build the Scarabs for Lance Reventlow, the well-built special featured a flathead Ford engine mounted in a tube frame. (Courtesy of Bill Haislett.)

Here, a mixed group of under 1,500-cc cars head down the straight at Pomona. Races at Pomona were held on a temporary course laid out in part on the Los Angeles County Fair Grounds parking lot and utilizing the famous drag strip there as a straight. (Courtesy of Bill Haislett.)

John Von Nuemann takes the traditional victory lap with a trophy girl as he waves to the camera at Pomona in his Ferrari Testarossa. Hollywood-based import car dealer Von Nuemann was one of the biggest supporters of road racing in the region. (Courtesy of Bill Haislett.)

Racing at Santa Barbara Municipal Airport in Goleta began in the early 1950s and was held twice yearly around the Memorial Day and Labor Day weekends. Popular with drivers and spectators alike, it was considered a fast course and the races there attracted large crowds until the late 1960s, when the expansion of airport business forced an end to the events. This aerial view gives an excellent idea of the course layout. The start/finish line is at center, with the big airplane hangar at turn one below and to its left. By the time this picture was taken in 1957, attendance was already high; in later years, it peaked at over 30,000. (Courtesy of Bill Haislett.)

This shot of the pits at Santa Barbara shows a nice line of Mercedes 300s plus Chuck Porter's SLS. At the end and seeming out of place among all that German metal is Max Balchowsky's Ol Yaller. Ina Balchowsky, Max's wife and an excellent mechanic in her own right, appears to be seated on the rear fender, wearing a white coat. (Courtesy of Bill Haislett.)

A mixed group of under 1,500-cc cars go around turn two at Santa Barbara, seemingly in the opposite direction that the races were usually held. The car closest to the camera, No. 32, is a Crosley special. Next to it on the left is a Nichols-Panhard. (Courtesy of Bill Haislett.)

Three veteran drivers battle it out while rounding turn eight at Santa Barbara in May 1960. In the lead is Jim Matthews driving a Buick-powered Aston Martin DB-3S, followed by Dick Morgensen in his Ferrari 250 Testarossa, and Cal Club president D.D. Michelmore in a Porsche Spyder. (Courtesy of John Masterson.)

Passing the hay bales around turn eight at Santa Barbara, Dick Brashears of Santa Barbara in the Ferrari Testarossa leads a Porsche 550 Spyder and a Porsche Cooper. The large crowd in the background gives some idea of the popularity of road racing in the early 1960s. (Courtesy of John Masterson.)

The crowd is on its feet as it watches emergency personnel pull an injured driver from his burning car at Santa Barbara. "Racing can be dangerous!" was a frequent slogan seen in race programs of the day, and fatalities at race meets were known to close down some tracks. (Courtesy of John Masterson.)

Johnny Von Neumann, in his Ferrari, is being hotly pursued by Duffy Livingstone in the "Eliminator" Model T roadster around turn eight at Santa Barbara. Livingstone and his old hot rod could always give the high-end sports cars a run for their money. (Courtesy of Bill Haislett.)

In this shot, Von Neumann (left) comes up alongside a Jaguar C-Type and a Siata while passing the officials' stand at Santa Barbara. Note the painting scaffold set up at center for photographers. (Courtesy of Bill Haislett.)

Willow Springs International Motorsports Park is located in the desert foothill country just north of Los Angeles. Designed by Bill Pollack and opened in 1953, it is California's oldest continuously operating racetrack. In this view from the parking lot, the main part of the two-and-a-half-mile track is visible in the center background (Courtesy of John Masterson.)

This shot shows the barren desert landscape that surrounds the track at Willow Springs as John Masterson, in the No. 222 "Batmobile," leads D.D. Michelmore in the Porsche RSK. The fact that there were no trees or other obstructions around the track made it safer to drive fast. (Courtesy of John Masterson.)

In the early days at Willow Springs, there was very little there besides the track, so racing teams and spectators alike had to improvise. This Masterson Motors VW Kombi was used as an impromptu viewing stand. (Courtesy of John Masterson.)

Willow Springs is a popular track, challenging, with well-designed curves and many ups and downs. In the lead here is John Masterson, with Chuck Cornett behind in the No. 143 Ferrari Monza and Ken Miles in the Von Nuemann Porsche RSK. This image is from the February 1960 Cal Club meet. (Courtesy of John Masterson.)

As can be seen in the background, this shot of Willow Springs from the 1980s shows the much-improved amenities for both drivers and spectators. Bill Haislett of Seal Beach, who took many of the photographs in this book, is piloting the No. 136 MGB in the center foreground. (Courtesy of Bill Haislett.)

Riverside International Speedway opened in 1957 and closed in 1989. Located in the arid desert foothills of the Moreno Valley, the track was a popular venue with drivers and crowds alike for many years. Designed and built by the West Coast Automotive Testing Corporation, the track's construction encountered financial difficulties and had the added misfortune of having a driver die in an accident during the first race. A definite challenge to drive, it eventually required the redesign of a very dangerous spot at turns one and nine. By the late 1980s, dwindling attendance and rising land values spelled doom for the speedway, and no trace of it remains today. Here, Richie Ginther drives one of Lance Reventlow's Scarabs to victory in a 1957 race. (Courtesy of Bill Haislett.)

Pete Woods speeds past the camera in his black-and-yellow Jaguar D-Type at Riverside on a practice day. Note the spectators and cars scattered around on the infield with no thought given to safety or security. (Courtesy of John Masterson.)

The orange-and-white No. 46 Corvette owned and driven by Walt Hansken charges through the redwoods at Pebble Beach. This photograph was taken during the last meet at the Pebble Beach race course, which was held on April 22, 1956. (Courtesy of John Masterson.)

Racing at Pebble Beach ended when popular driver Ernie McAfee was killed while racing there in 1956. By 1957, a group of Monterey area enthusiasts and businessmen had succeeded in building a new 2.2-mile track on a part of the Fort Ord military reservation. Located in the same type of coastal foothill terrain as the Paramount Ranch track but of superior design, Laguna Seca was quickly recognized as a world-class track by the racing community. This shot shows a pack rounding turn nine during a 1963 Grand Prix qualifying race. (Courtesy of John Masterson.)

A pair of Lotus 7 roadsters have a mix-up on a hot, dusty day at Laguna Seca. The car in the foreground appears to be taking evasive action. The location is at the top of the hill leading into the famous downhill "corkscrew" at turns eight and eight A. (Courtesy of John Masterson.)

The road course at Laguna Seca is so well designed that automobile manufacturers have long used it as a test track, a practice that continues today. Here, in 1963, a Chevrolet Corvette Stingray experimental prototype is being put through its paces. Note the side exhaust pipes. (Courtesy of John Masterson.)

Although outside Southern California, a track that was located in Cotati, California, in Sonoma County, is worth a mention. Like so many other race venues, it utilized an abandoned military installation; in this case, a naval airfield. This shot shows a Lotus 11 passing the start/finish line. (Courtesy of John Masterson.)

Racing activity at Cotati began around 1956 when a local enthusiast group, the Racing Drivers Club, began using it for club meets and as a practice track. The first SCCA race was held there in May 1957. Here, Al Norman in a Lotus 18 passes a fair-sized crowd between turns eight and nine. (Courtesy of John Masterson.)

Being situated in Northern California, races held in springtime at Cotati were subject to sudden rainstorms, causing headaches for many drivers. Here, the unidentified driver of a BMC Formula Junior pushes his car off the wet track after spinning out. (Courtesy of John Masterson)

On a rainy day at Cotati in February 1964, two flagmen relax after sweeping up a broken hay bale and watch a homemade race car speed past on a qualifying lap. The little special seen here was powered by a Mercury 650 outboard boat motor mounted sideways behind the driver. (Courtesy of John Masterson.)

Seen in the pits at Cotati during a May 1963 race is Jerry Titus's Chevrolet Corvair–powered Huffaker Genie sports car, which must have been brand new at the time this picture was taken. When the SCCA, which had previously been oriented toward the amateur racer, began staging professional races in 1963, it opened the door for car builders like Joe Huffaker to create larger, faster cars with no limitations on engine size. The Mk 8 model pictured here usually mounted a 215-ci Buick V8, so the Corvair installation seen here is rather unusual. Note the generally excellent quality of the fit and finish. (Both, courtesy of John Masterson.)

Four

THE CARS

The whole world of road racing revolved around one thing, the sports car, which was still a novelty in mid-century America. The term "sports car" is rather nebulous, but basically describes a small-wheelbase, (under 95 inches) two-passenger car that has quick acceleration and good road handling and would be considered fun to drive. In road racing, there were two classes of sports cars, production or stock, and modified. Stock meant just that; stock from the factory with no added parts. Engine bore and stroke could not be changed, but tuning tweaks like camshaft grinding were permitted. Modified was a different matter entirely. Anything was permissible as long as the car conformed to basic requirements like having two seats and possessing vestigial fenders, headlights, and taillights. Seen here is Carl Shipman and his Allard J2 in the inspection line at Willow Springs. (Courtesy of Joel Driskill.)

Stirling Edwards was a prominent San Francisco industrialist and sportsman who was interested in motorsports of all kinds, particularly road racing. He had a sports special, seen here, custom built in 1950. Norman Timbs designed the aluminum body, which Edwards had the firm of Diedt and Lesovsky fabricate. The heavy tube frame was based on a BMW, featured independent front and rear suspension, and carried a 153-ci Ford V8 60 built by Eddie Meyer. The little special proved to be an excellent sports car, easily convertible from street driving to racing. It is seen here in 1951 at the first annual Palm Springs Road Race, where it won first place. (Both, courtesy of Joel Driskill.)

The second Edwards Special is seen here at Torrey Pines in 1952. A completely different design, it had a Chrysler engine mounted in a modified Henry J frame with a fiberglass body. Utilizing other Henry J parts as well, it had many bugs and was not successful. (Courtesy of Joel Driskill.)

This is what appears to be a very early pre-A Porsche 356 Carrera, seen in the paddock at Riverside. The light blue metallic coupe sports red, white, and blue racing stripes, stone guards over the headlights, and a candy-striped dowel propping up the hood. (Courtesy of John Masterson.)

This Devin-Panhard is seen at Goleta. Devin-Panhards were built by Bill Devin at his garage/factory in El Monte, California. Powered by highly modified Panhard 750 and 850 air-cooled engines with front-wheel-drive transaxles and mounted on a Devin-designed ladder frame, they were covered by a fiberglass body based on the 1953 Deutsch-Bonnet LeMans racer. (Courtesy of John Masterson.)

Dick Brashear's rare and iconic Ferrari 250 Testa Rossa Spyder is seen here in the pits at Goleta. The hood has been removed to expose the 3-liter V12 engine, including the famous red-painted valve covers. Note the long line of carburetor intakes. (Courtesy of John Masterson.)

A trio of Triumph Spitfires sweeps around the track at Goleta. The 1,100-cc, 67-horsepower Michelotti-designed Spitfire was intended to compete with the low-end MG Midgets and Austin-Healey Sprites that were flooding the American sports car market. Introduced in 1962, it was a big success and became a common sight on the streets of Southern California. (Courtesy of Joe Danely.)

Johnny Von Nuemann displays his customary driving style as he drifts his Ferrari Monza through a curve at Paramount Ranch. The car pictured here appears to be a 750 series from 1954, powered by a 3.0-liter four-cylinder engine generating 250 horsepower. (Courtesy of Bill Haislett.)

No. 55, a Lotus 11 driven by Ed Freutel of San Marino, passes the camera as spectators watch in the background at Paramount Ranch. Distinctively styled Lotus 11s, also called the LeMans, were usually powered by Coventry Climax engines although owners fitted a wide range of other makes like Maserati, DKW, and Saab. (Courtesy of Bill Haislett.)

The legendary 1,098-cc Coventry Climax FWA engine that powered the Lotus is seen here. Originally designed to power a water pump, the FWA was incredibly light at around 180 pounds and produced 75 horsepower. Coventry Climax engines were also used in Coopers and in Formula One cars. (Courtesy of Bill Haislett.)

While the adults have their backs turned, a pair of boys take the opportunity to examine Bill Pollack's Corvette-Lister at Riverside. The beautifully aerodynamic Chevrolet-powered Lister was already obsolete when it was introduced in 1958, as it was becoming clear that rear-engine cars like the Cooper were the future. (Courtesy of Bill Haislett.)

Bill Murphy's red and white Kurtis-Buick, seen here at Santa Barbara in 1960, was a familiar sight at California road races during the late 1950s. Murphy, a Culver City Buick dealer, was heavily involved in the sport. His driver during this meet was veteran racer and designer of the Willow Springs race course, Bill Pollack. (Courtesy of Bill Haislett.)

Bob Drake speeds past the camera in Joe Lubin's Cooper T39 Bobtail. Powered by a Coventry Climax 1500 engine, the beautifully streamlined T39 was introduced at Goodwood in 1955. A very successful design, Cooper Bobtails participated on tracks all over the world and gave rival Lotus a serious run for its money. (Courtesy of Bill Haislett.)

It looks like Bob Drake in the Cooper is about to get into some trouble as his left front wheel begins to leave the pavement. Englishman Ken Miles in the Porsche 550 and Australian driver Robbie Robinson in the No. 77 MGA have him boxed in as well. Note the nasty-looking gully just up ahead. (Courtesy of Bill Haislett.)

Von Neumann's Porsche 550 RS, with Ken Miles behind the wheel, hurtles around a curve. Johnny Von Neumann owned the famous Competition Motors in Hollywood and is considered the man most responsible for the popularity of the Porsche make, first in California, and then in the rest of the country. He was also an early advocate for Ferrari. (Courtesy of Bill Haislett.)

AC Cars of England was another rare marque frequently seen on California race courses. This version of the AC Ace roadster, known as an AC Bristol, was powered by a 2,000-cc six-cylinder engine produced by Bristol Cars. When Bristol quit supplying engines, AC went to American racer Carrol Shelby for installation of Ford's 289 V8, and the result was the world famous AC Shelby Cobra. (Courtesy of Bill Haislett.)

The mid-engine Porsche 550 RS, first raced at the famous Nürburgring track in Germany, debuted in 1953. By 1957, when this photograph was taken, it had been surpassed by the more advanced 718 RSK model. The 550 is perhaps most famous as the type that actor James Dean drove to his death in 1955. (Courtesy of Bill Haislett.)

Only 90 of the Porsche RS series were made, and it seems most were raced in California at one time or another. Although most were seen in the factory-issued silver color, this attractive red and white example enters the camera's frame at Paramount Ranch. (Courtesy of Bill Haislett.)

Racing great Dan Gurney's red 4.9-liter Ferrari, No. 88, is seen parked next to Joe Lubin's Cooper at Pomona. A big, powerful car, the Ferrari 4.9 could be a brute to drive and was wickedly unforgiving. The Lampredi-designed V12 engine in Gurney's Ferrari produced around 340 horsepower. (Courtesy of Bill Haislett.)

The 283-ci V8 engine that most Corvettes were equipped with supplied more than enough horsepower to make them competitive in a road race. How they handled at speed was another matter, as can be seen by this 'Vette taking to the dirt at Pomona. The driver appears to be John Masterson of Ventura, California. (Courtesy of Bill Haislett.)

The Talbot Lago Grand Prix racer owned by Bob Estes and Otto Zipper made an appearance in the pits at Pomona during the August 1957 meet, although it didn't compete. Built by an Anglo-French company, the Talbot Lago, while not particularly fast, was reliable and managed to come in first at Le Mans in 1951 because of it. (Courtesy of Bill Haislett.)

The cream of European sports cars, like this Ferrari Berlinetta, could be seen in the parking lots of tracks like Pomona and Riverside. Loaded with chrome trim and sporting a pair of fog lamps, exotics like the Berlinetta were frequent sights on the streets of Beverly Hills and along the Sunset Strip in the late 1950s. (Courtesy of Bill Haislett.)

The most distinctive feature of the Mercedes 300 SL was its gull-wing doors. Stylistically unusual and modernistic, the upward-swinging doors were designed to clear the car's tubular frame. This example was parked in the lot at Pomona during the August 1957 meet. (Courtesy of Bill Haislett.)

This Jaguar D-Type, driven by Hollywood resident Jack Douglas, squats in its parking space in the pits during the Labor Day 1956 meet at Santa Barbara. In the background are two Porsche speedsters, Gary Nelson's No. 318, and No. 180, owned by Jay Hills of Beverly Hills. (Courtesy of Bill Haislett.)

This is Bill Krause and his Jaguar D-Type in action at Santa Barbara. Although largely forgotten today, Krause was known as an extremely skilled and competitive driver who earned the respect of peers like Moss, Brabham, and Gurney. He would later race for Carroll Shelby. (Courtesy of Bill Haislett.)

Here is Krause's Jaguar seen from the front, showing its attractive paint scheme to good advantage. It was powered by the factory-supplied 3.4-liter DOHC six, later bored out to 3.8 liters. In the right background is No. 79, an MG Special owned and driven by John Sousa of Alhambra. (Courtesy of Bill Haislett.)

Don Hulette and his blue ex-Pickford Jaguar Special were a common sight at race tracks in California during the late 1950s. Hulette replaced the Jaguar XK engine with a Chevrolet 283 V8 that turned the Special into a real frontrunner. (Courtesy of Bill Haislett.)

This interesting Volkswagen Beetle pickup conversion was created by Bakersfield-based P&S Motors. Pressed into service transporting traffic cones to the far reaches of the racetrack, it is seen at the start/finish line at Santa Barbara as various racing types mill around. (Courtesy of Bill Haislett.)

A rare Moretti sports car made an appearance in the pits during the Labor Day 1956 meet at Santa Barbara, although it did not compete. Morettis were built in Turin, Italy, and featured a four-cylinder 750-cc twin-cam engine that produced 58 horsepower. (Courtesy of Bill Haislett.)

SCCA official and actor John Timanus's Lotus 8 is seen in the Santa Barbara pits with the big hangar at turns one and two visible at upper left. "Dusty" Miller's MG special sits behind it, and in the background are a couple of Formula racers being prepared for an upcoming race. (Courtesy of Bill Haislett.)

This is an OSCA MT4 owned by George and Myra Buchanan and driven by Myra Buchanan. OSCA was founded in 1947 when the Maserati brothers left the company bearing their name (industrialist Adolfi Orso actually owned the Maserati brand), to build their own cars again. The MT4 was produced from 1948 to 1959 and had a number of different engines and bodies. (Courtesy of Bill Haislett.)

The 1,498-cc engine that powered the Porsche Spyders of the 1950s were used in other applications as well. When mounted in a Cooper frame and body, like the "Riviera Special" owned by T.R. Corazza, seen here, the results were irreverently called "Poopers," as in Porsche-Cooper. (Courtesy of Bill Haislett.)

A Porsche engine found its way into this Lotus 9 owned by Dr. William Estrich of Burbank. Seen here at Santa Barbara in September 1956, this one is notable because the engine was the one that was in the Porsche Spyder actor James Dean was driving when he was killed in a head-on collision at Cholame, California, on September 30, 1955. CSCC member Joe Playan remembers that the engine was purchased by Estrich, who later wrecked the car. Dr. Troy McHenry of Beverly Hills bought some of the suspension parts for his Porsche and was killed in it at Pomona. The transmission was installed in yet another car, which was also involved in a fatal crash. (Both, courtesy of Bill Haislett.)

Over 17,000 Alfa Romeo Giulietta Spyders were built, with a large number of them going to California. The iconic body design was produced by the famed firm Pininfarina and epitomized the typical Italian sports car of the 1950s and 1960s. (Courtesy of Bill Haislett.)

The 1,290-cc engine in the Giulietta produced 100 horsepower, which made it quite competitive in the under 1,500 cc races. This one, prepared for racing by Jack Brumby and Frank Aldhous and driven by Rey Martinez, is seen rounding turn five at Paramount Ranch. (Courtesy of Bill Haislett.)

Australian Robbie Robinson climbs up the grade coming out of turn five at Paramount Ranch in the No. 77 Gough Industries MGA. Gough Industries was an early importer of MG cars and foreign car parts. The MGA seen here, while raced as a stock production car, actually was specially tuned for racing and had quite an edge over the competition. (Courtesy of Bill Haislett.)

Bill Krause is driving Jack Brumby's Maserati 450S to second place during the 1959 SCCA meet at Pomona. One of two imported to the United States, the 4.5-liter V8-powered thoroughbred was also raced by Carroll Shelby and Jim Hall. (Courtesy of Bill Haislett.)

The British-built Cooper Climax T43, seen here at Pomona in 1959, was a revelation to most American drivers when it appeared on the scene in the 1950s. The combination of the lightweight and powerful Climax engine and excellent handling characteristics inherent in the rear engine design of the Cooper sparked a revolution in how American race cars were made and led to the end of front-engine cars in road and formula racing. (Courtesy of John Masterson.)

Here is a shot of Augie Pabst Jr.'s ultra-exotic Scarab racer "Meister Brauser 1" being prepared by the pit crew at Riverside. The Pabst family name is associated with three generations of road racing in California, starting with SCCA champion driver Augie Pabst Sr. and winding up with Augie Pabst III, an accomplished driver in Can-Am, Formula Continental, and Formula Ford racing. (Courtesy of John Masterson.)

Scarab race cars were superb machines when they were built in the late 1950s, but their front-engine configuration was already on the road to obsolescence. After an unsuccessful try at Formula One racing, Scarab owner Lance Reventlow had his designers Tom Barnes and Dick Troutman build him the mid-engine sports car seen above. Powered by a Buick V8, the new Scarab is seen making its debut at the Labor Day 1962 meet at Santa Barbara. The car performed well, coming in second and running a very competitive race. Reventlow ran it at a few more meets before losing interest in road racing altogether. The car was eventually sold to Augie Pabst, who still owns it today. (Both, courtesy of John Masterson.)

Reventlow's mid-engine Scarab is seen here in the pits at Santa Barbara. Undeniably a beautiful car, the design had great potential, and it was a pity when Reventlow chose to cease production. The Reventlow Automobiles plant in Venice, California, was sold to Carroll Shelby, who moved his Shelby-American Motors there to produce the Cobra Mustang for Ford. The mid-engine car seen here was first sold to John Mecom Jr. of Texas, who replaced the Buick power plant with a 327-ci Chevrolet. A.J. Foyt drove it for Mecom during the 1963 season with moderate success, and Walt Hansgen drove it to a single first-place win in 1964 before it was sold to Augie Pabst, who still owns it. Lance Reventlow was killed in a plane crash in 1971. (Courtesy of John Masterson.)

The mid-engine Campbell Special seen here at Santa Barbara in September 1962 was developed by fiberglass boat manufacturer Bill Campbell. Campbell was a veteran lake racer and successful businessman with the resources to build his own race car, and he spared no expense. Indy car builder Wayne Ewing designed and built the tube frame, and an 1,100-cc JAP motorcycle engine supplied the power. A 283-ci Corvette V8 soon replaced the JAP, and along with beefed up suspension, the lightweight, perfectly-balanced race car saw its first victory in the June 1962 meet at Riverside. This photograph (with Bob Drake behind the wheel) was taken a few minutes before the Special was nearly destroyed in a spectacular non-fatal crash. It has been rebuilt several times over the years. (Courtesy of John Masterson.)

Dave MacDonald and the Corvette he drove for Don Steves Chevrolet of La Habra were popular sights at Southern California road races in the early 1960s. Don Steves owned a large Chevrolet dealership and enthusiastically raced Corvettes throughout the Southland, founding the Corvette Super Sports Club in 1959. (Courtesy of John Masterson.)

The glamorous Maserati Tipo 61 "Birdcage" made frequent appearances at tracks in the Southland. Powered by a 2.9-liter four-cylinder rated at 250 horsepower, it was quick but notoriously unreliable. (Courtesy of John Masterson.)

Besides sports cars, Formula Junior races were held during most Southern California club meets by the late 1950s. Begun in 1958 as a low-cost way for enthusiasts to enter the sport of open-wheel formula racing, the cars were required to use production-based engines, transmissions, and brakes. The requirements were fairly strict but gave the amateur home mechanic a chance to build a race car economically. Soon, however, constructors like Stanguellini and Elva were producing turnkey Formula Junior race cars. As the sport grew in popularity, the British marques Cooper and Lotus began to produce highly successful cars as well. In a few years, Formula Junior racers grew so sophisticated and expensive that the amateur could no longer afford to compete. Eventually absorbed into Formula Two and Three racing, the concept reappeared later as Formula Ford and Vee. (Courtesy of John Masterson.)

The Lotus 20, seen here leading an unidentified rear engine special around the turn at Santa Barbara, was powered by a modified engine from a Ford Cortina saloon. Lotus produced some of the most aesthetically pleasing designs in motorsports. (Courtesy of John Masterson.)

An early Formula Junior type was the Elva 100, which commonly used BMC A-Series engines, a type found in many British production cars. The example seen here is being driven by Norm Babcock and was owned by Barry Atsatt, a Santa Barbara Elva dealer. (Courtesy of John Masterson.)

The OSCA FJ 1100 was introduced in 1959 and was the Maserati brothers' entry into the world of Formula Junior racing. Although OSCA manufactured its own four-cylinder overhead-cam engines of various sizes, the FJ 1100 used a 1,089-cc Fiat unit. (Courtesy of John Masterson.)

The T59 Mk 3 Formula Junior was Cooper's 1962 entry into the field. Motive power came from a 1,095-cc BMC-XSP engine. The T59 Mk3 was very popular with American race drivers, and this example is seen being raced in the Labor Day 1962 meet at Santa Barbara. (Courtesy of John Masterson.)

Ventura County Volkswagen dealer John Masterson used this Westphalia camper van as one of the support vehicles as his racing team traveled from track to track across California. Being the largest VW dealer in the region, Masterson was able to put together a caravan consisting of two "Westies" and a Kombi pickup as well. (Courtesy of John Masterson.)

The Kurtis Kraft 500S was a sports car that was available either ready to drive from the factory or in kit form. Based in Glendale, California, Kurtis Kraft manufactured midget racers and was famous as a builder of Indianapolis cars. The 500S was available with a variety of V8 engines. (Courtesy of John Masterson.)

Two Mini Coopers negotiate a fast turn at Laguna Seca with ease while the 1964 Ford Futura Sprint at right is about to get into trouble. While the Ford's optional 260-ci V8 could produce 164 horsepower, its handling was no match for the nimble front-wheel-drive Mini. (Courtesy of Barry Atsatt.)

The Porsche 356 gained the company its reputation as a world-class manufacturer of sports cars. Seen here at Santa Barbara is a 356 A Super Spyder variant. Spyders were supplied with the special four-cam Carrera racing engine, which later became available as an option on production cars. (Courtesy of John Masterson.)

Three "Bug Eye" Sprites kick up some dust at Santa Barbara during a race for production cars under 1,000 cc. The Austin Healy (actually British Motor Corporation) Sprite was powered by the ubiquitous Austin A Series 948-cc engine, used in many a British sport and passenger car. (Courtesy of John Masterson.)

Santa Barbara Elva dealer Barry Atsatt attended the 1960 12 Hours of Sebring race with the Elva team. While he was there, he took this picture of the OSCA S750 that Americans John Bently and John Gordon drove to 12th place. (Courtesy of Barry Atsatt.)

One of the most interesting cars back in the golden age was Chuck Porter's Mercedes "SLS." Hollywood garage owner Porter paid $500 for a new Mercedes SL Gullwing that had been totally wrecked and burned while being delivered. Scrapping the twisted steel body and laboriously straightening the frame, he had an aluminum body crafted by Hollywood coachbuilder Jack Sutton to closely resemble the Mercedes SLR race cars. Porter rebuilt and slightly tuned the original Mercedes 3-liter engine, although he soon replaced it with a series of American V8s. The SLS (S standing for "scrap"), as it became known, and Porter were popular attractions at California speedways throughout the late 1950s and early 1960s. (Courtesy of Bill Haislett.)

John "Bat" Masterson's Batmobile, pictured here at Willow Springs in 1960, is a typical example of the type of custom-built specials seen on West Coast race tracks during the golden age. Having previously raced a stock Corvette, Masterson wanted something more competitive and went about having his own built. He can be seen leaning hard on the brakes as he slows the big special down. (Photograph by James La Tourette.)

Masterson purchased a special from Reno-based racer Merle Brennan that had been dubbed the "Beast" because of its rough appearance. The car was stripped down to its tube frame, which began life in a sprint car, and was sent to the garage of Santa Barbara engine master Bob Joehnck. The frame can be seen at left in this image. (Courtesy of John Masterson.)

Joehnck's garage was and still is a legend to Central Coast hot rodders, having produced the engines and cars for many of the biggest names in racing. Joehnck is seen standing at center. As the racer was being assembled, Masterson and Joehnck had decided on a new Corvette 327 as the engine. (Courtesy of John Masterson.)

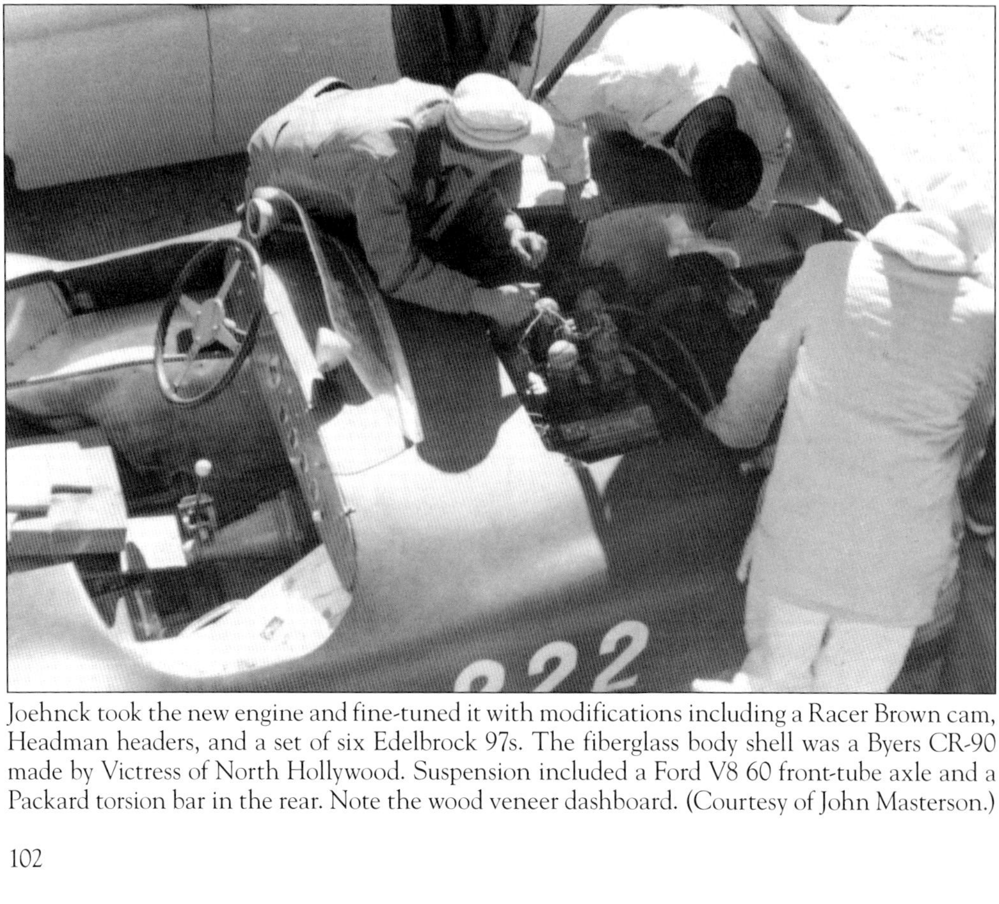

Joehnck took the new engine and fine-tuned it with modifications including a Racer Brown cam, Headman headers, and a set of six Edelbrock 97s. The fiberglass body shell was a Byers CR-90 made by Victress of North Hollywood. Suspension included a Ford V8 60 front-tube axle and a Packard torsion bar in the rear. Note the wood veneer dashboard. (Courtesy of John Masterson.)

Here, Masterson and the Batmobile cut inside another American-built sports car, a Devin SS. Built by fiberglass car body pioneer Bill Devin at his factory in El Monte, California, the SS was offered fully assembled with a tube frame and powered by a Chevrolet 283 for around $10,000 in 1964. The Devin SS was known for the high quality of its fit and finish. (Photograph by James La Tourette.)

Here is a nice shot of a Kurtis 500 being loaded onto its trailer. Manufactured in the Glendale, California, factory belonging to Midget and Indy car builder Frank Kurtis, the 500 was a fairly common sight at Southland speedways and a good, inexpensive way to get into racing. Available fully assembled or as a kit, it could mount a wide variety of American V8 engines. (Photograph by James La Tourette.)

Max Balchowsky's original Ol Yaller leads Ken Miles in the Porsche Spyder up the hill to turn five at Paramount Ranch. The name "Ol Yaller" was used on a series of at least nine specials built and raced by Hollywood garage owner Max Balchowsky. The version seen here, referred to as the Mk One, was actually built in Arizona by Dick Morgenson and Boyd Hough and raced there and in New Mexico successfully. Balchowsky bought the Morgenson Special, as it was known, in 1954. The special was reportedly built up from pieces of a Jaguar XK-120 and powered by a Plymouth 217-ci inline six. After a few races, Balchowsky replaced the six with a Buick V8. It is seen here being driven by Eric Hauser to first place at the September 1957 Cal Club meet. (Courtesy of Bill Haislett.)

Here, Ol Yaller Mk Two crowds a Ferrari Testarossa at Pomona. Referred to by Balchowsky as a "Buick-Kurtis," it did use most of the parts from a Kurtis 500 kit but was built using many modifications that Max and his wife, Ina (a fine mechanic in her own right), devised. (Courtesy of Bill Hiaslett.)

In this long shot, Eric Hauser speeds past the crowd down the long drag-strip straight at Pomona. According to legend, Balchowsky laid out and arranged the frame rails and other parts of the Mk Two on his garage floor until "it looked right," and Ina then jotted down the dimensions for assembly. (Courtesy of Bill Haislett.)

Racing great Roger Penske Jr. is seen here at Laguna Seca driving one of the original Chaparral 2 racers. This groundbreaking car was the first of a new breed of American race car that was built using scientific data more than experience gained on the garage floor. (Courtesy of John Masterson.)

On October 18, 1964, Penske climbs the hill before turn six at Laguna Seca during a qualifying session. The Chaparral series of race cars were designed and built by a Cal Tech–trained engineer, oilman, and race car driver from Texas named Jim Hall and his partner, Hap Sharp, who together formed Chaparral Cars. (Courtesy of John Masterson.)

Hall and Sharp had bought one of Troutman and Barnes's front-engine Chaparral race cars (which they were building after having left Scarab), and after doing extensive modifications, decided to design and build their own car. This photograph, taken on May 10, 1964, at Kent, Washington, shows No. 66, which was driven by Jim Hall, and No. 67, driven by Hap Sharp. (Courtesy of John Masterson.)

Here, Penske overtakes a Genie in a Chaparral 2A. The 2A can be identified by the aerodynamic vanes visible just forward of the front wheel on the car's body. These were adjustable via a pedal by the driver's left foot and were used to help hold the front end down on the straights. Also note the Kammback rear body, another aerodynamic feature of the car's advanced design. (Courtesy of John Masterson.)

Jim Hall, a trained engineer and experienced driver, knew exactly what he wanted in a race car and had the means to build one. Along with Hap Sharp, he was also able to enlist extensive covert aid from Chevrolet and the General Motors research and development department. Allowed access to early computer data on the aerodynamics relating to suspension and handling from GM, as well as being well supplied with engines, automatic transmissions, (another first in race cars) and other crucial parts, the new Chaparral 2 took the racing world by storm. The image below shows details of the 327-ci first-generation small-block engine, six Weber carbs, and rear suspension. (Both, courtesy of John Masterson.)

The spartan cockpit of a Chaparral 2 was all business. To the left is the tachometer, and below it, the oil pressure gauge. To the right of the steering wheel are the coolant temperature gauge and the power and headlight switches. Note the battery at lower right. (Courtesy of John Masterson.)

The Cooper T61 Monaco, seen here at Laguna Seca, took the frame design for Cooper's Formula One car and beefed it up to accommodate a Ford V8. Cooper Monacos were driven by Roger Penske Jr. and Carroll Shelby, who used the Cooper Monaco as a base for the "King Cobra" supercars. (Courtesy of John Masterson.)

Here is a little roadster called the Nardi-Crosley, seen at Santa Barbara in the late 1950s. The Nardi was built in Italy using Fiat parts attached to a tube frame covered by a Ferrari Monza–inspired body by Bertone. The engine was the American made Crosley 724-cc overhead-cam inline four. (Courtesy of John Masterson.)

This image of a Nardi-Crosley in action at Vacaville, California, gives some idea of the sports car's small size. The Crosley engine was originally designed as an auxiliary power unit for uses such as pumps, generators, and large aircraft electrical systems. (Courtesy of John Masterson.)

Another largely forgotten American made sports car was the Cheetah. Only 11 examples were built in 1963 by race driver and Corvette specialist Bill Thomas in Anaheim, California. Conceived by Thomas as a Corvette-powered rival to Carroll Shelby's Cobra Mustang, the Cheetah never received support from GM for development, and Thomas was forced to quit producing them due to lack of resources. The 90-inch wheelbase Cheetah was powered by a fuel-injected 327-ci Corvette V8 and four-speed transmission. The transmission output shaft connected directly to the differential through a universal joint; the car's small size made it impossible to use a conventional drive shaft. (Both, courtesy of John Masterson.)

Driver A.T. Whatley is seen here in a Ford GT40 Mk 1 at Santa Barbara during a September race. The GT40 was a result of Henry Ford II's desire to build a race car that would win the 24 Hours of Le Mans. Having been frustrated in his attempt to buy Ferrari, Ford turned to the Ford Advanced Vehicles Division located in Slough, United Kingdom, to design and build a long-distance sports car that could not only win Le Mans, but also put Ferrari in its place. The 1964 Mk 1 pictured here was powered by a 289-ci Ford Fairlane V8, and from the looks of it, had already done a lot of hard racing when this picture was taken. The GT40 became so popular that Ford has produced the Ford GT sports car as a modern tribute. (Both, courtesy of Joe Danely.)

The AC Shelby Cobra was a big hit with the public when introduced in 1963, and copies of one kind or another are still being produced today. The one seen here is a Mk 2, equipped with a Ford Windsor 289-ci V8, attending the 1964 Aerojet safety run. (Courtesy of John Masterson.)

To gain credibility as a serious race car, Shelby campaigned the Cobra at road races up and down the West Coast. The driver was none other than Ken Miles, who had gotten famous driving Porsches for John Von Neumann. Here, a Cobra bearing Miles's race number, 50, is being unloaded from the Shelby trailer at Kent, Washington, in 1964. (Courtesy of John Masterson.)

The bare-bones Lotus 7 was a relatively inexpensive way to get into racing. Built in the United Kingdom by Colin Chapman's Lotus Engineering Company, the 7 was powered by a 1,498-cc Cosworth engine. After selling over 3,000 of the 7, Lotus sold the design to Caterham Cars, which has kept it in production to this day. (Courtesy of John Masterson.)

The other end of the spectrum for Lotus was the beautiful Elite. The nimble little fiberglass-bodied sports coupe had a Coventry Climax engine under the hood. This one is seen at Santa Barbara with another Lotus product in the right background: a Lotus 20 Formula Junior car. (Courtesy of John Masterson.)

Obsolescence is the sad but inevitable fate of all race cars as advances in technology produce ever faster machines. This group of older front-engine "big cars," including many veterans of the Indianapolis 500, are seen competing in the Sacramento 100, a minor race held at the Sacramento Fairgrounds in 1964. Old names like Kurtis and Offenhauser were in the past, as new ones like Lotus and Cooper became famous. Most of the cars seen here were soon stored away in garages and museums. (Both, courtesy of John Masterson.)

Dashboards are the control center of a race car, and it is interesting to see the different approaches designers use. This Cooper Monaco has a simple flat panel with the tachometer and engine gauges loosely arrayed around the simple steering wheel, with the various electrical switches on either side. The lack of upholstery makes much of the car's structure visible. (Courtesy of John Masterson.)

This Ferrari Testarossa from the 1950s takes a more traditional street car approach. The tachometer and other gauges are tightly clustered under a cowling above the wood-trimmed steering wheel with the switches scattered across the dash. Both cars sport humorous plaques added to the dashboards that reflected the owner's personality. (Courtesy of John Masterson.)

By 1966, when this photograph was taken, road racing had evolved into a serious sport with professional and semipro classes. The casual amateur who took his daily driver to race on the weekend was pretty much gone by then. This much-modified Alfa Romeo Giulietta is seen during one of the last races held at Santa Barbara. (Courtesy of Joe Danely.)

Porsche's mid-1960s race car was the mid-engine 904 RSK sports coupe. Having focused on Formula One racing during the early 1960s, the 904 was a re-entry into sports car racing for Porsche. It was powered by a 2-liter flat-four engine, although some were built with the 911 flat-six. (Courtesy of Joe Danely.)

Talented veterans like Dale Tholen, seen here getting into trouble with his Thundermug Special, were still on the tracks in 1966. Tholen was part of a rare fraternity of builder/drivers dedicated to tuning the Crosley 724-cc engine, one of which powered the Thundermug. (Courtesy of Joe Danely.)

Dale Tholen had built a Crosley-powered sports car that was the scourge of the H-class races throughout the state in the late 1950s. In 1960, he built this fiberglass-bodied H modified special. After trying an unsuccessful custom-made engine, he installed a Crosley. The Crosley-powered special still exists today. (Courtesy of Joe Danely.)

Formula racing was still popular in the mid-1960s. This Lindquist Saab FJ driven by Rick Padock is out of the race as the left rear wheel becomes detached, taking the exhaust with it. Flagmen can be seen in the upper background as one rushes to the driver's aid while the other stands ready with a fire extinguisher. (Courtesy of Joe Danely.)

Ingvar Lindquist was a Southern California Saab dealer and avid racing fanatic with a history of racing in Saab-powered H-class production cars and modified specials. He turned to Formula racing in the early 1960s and no doubt took a dim view of the treatment his car was receiving on the day this photograph was taken. (Courtesy of Joe Danely.)

This unfortunate Sunbeam Tiger also did not finish the race, as it rolls over on the track at Santa Barbara. Fortunately for the driver, the substantial roll bar required by safety regulations—as well as seat belts and a helmet—prevented any serious injury. (Courtesy of Joe Danely.)

Here, a crowd surrounds the Tiger after it has been pushed off the track. The driver, Ed Barker, is standing at left center still wearing his helmet while a concerned individual at center, possibly owner Sherm Allen of Hermosa Beach, rushes up to inspect the damage. (Courtesy of Joe Danely.)

The mid-1960s saw more American cars competing in production-class road races. Chevrolet Corvettes had been on the racing scene since the mid-1950s, and soon, Ford Mustangs, introduced in late 1964 and one of the biggest successes in automotive history, began appearing on race tracks as well. This one is driven by Ray Wolff for Hi-Performance Motors of El Segundo, California. (Courtesy of Joe Danely.)

The high-performance options available to Mustang owners were endless, and individual dealerships offered their own custom performance packages tailored to whatever kind of racing buyers desired. This is a custom Mustang GT driven by Bob James for Cutter Ford, a North Hollywood dealership. (Courtesy of Joe Danely.)

The Falcon was Ford's economy compact base model and was designed as cheap transportation. A performance model, the Futura Sprint became available in 1964 equipped with a 260-ci V8 and sharing several components with the Mustang. Driving his own Falcon is Pete Cordts of San Gabriel, California. (Courtesy of Joe Danely.)

The 1964 Plymouth Barracuda was not really a sports car. More of a sporty-appearing subcompact, it nonetheless handled tolerably well and came with a surprising number of speed and suspension options. This example was owned and driven by Howard Lomazoff of Los Gatos, California. (Courtesy of Joe Danely.)

Jerry Entin of Beverly Hills passes the camera in his Olds-powered McLaren Elva M1A. Designed by New Zealand driver/engineer Bruce McLaren and built by Elva in the United Kingdom, 24 of the mid-engine sports cars were built, typically powered by Chevrolet 350-ci small blocks. (Courtesy of Joe Danely.)

Bob Challman of Hermosa Beach, California, had a long history as a driver for Lotus, beginning with the Lotus 7. Here, he is at Santa Barbara in 1966 driving another superb creation by Colin Chapman, the Lotus 23. Most 23s were powered by Cosworth four-cylinder engines in displacements beginning at 997 cc and eventually reaching 1,594 cc. (Courtesy of Joe Danely.)

In between races during the 1966 Santa Barbara meet, some local VIPs were given a ride around the track in a pair of Ferraris. This is a 250 MM, a production version of the car that won the 1952 Mille Miglia (Thousand Miles) endurance race in Italy. (Courtesy of Joe Danely.)

This is a 1964 Ferrari 250 GT Lusso Berlinetta. The GT Lusso was a long-distance luxury tourer derived from the Tour de France–winning short wheel base 250 GT SWB. A relative success for Ferrari with 350 being sold, the sleek tourer's body was designed by Pininfarina. (Courtesy of Joe Danely.)

The unidentified driver of this Lotus 7 has wound up sitting across the roadway at Santa Barbara. Since no Lotus 7s appear on the program for this meet, the car seen here was either a late entry, or this photograph was taken during the practice or qualifying runs before the race. (Courtesy of Joe Danely.)

A spectator wistfully inspects Barry Atsatt's Elva Formula Junior while John Masterson (in white shirt) stands by his Porsche RSK. Note the battery and fuel-tank installation on the Elva. (Courtesy of John Masterson.)

Road races were a chance for sports cars enthusiasts to gather and celebrate their sport. Here, in this early 1960s photograph taken near turn eight at Santa Barbara, a happy crew gathers around a Volkswagen Westphalia camper van as a participant salutes the cameraman with a cool beverage. (Courtesy of John Masterson.)

Shown here is the equipment that the typical road-racing enthusiast needed for a day at the races: a folding chair, an 8mm movie camera (at right on fender) a ukulele for after race entertainment, and a generous supply of liquid refreshment. (Courtesy of John Masterson.)

This final image is a good representation of California's road-racing scene back in the golden age of motorsports. An Italian-built Alfa Romeo Special powered by a very American Cadillac 331-ci V8, owned by Hollywood personality and actor Keenan Wynn and driven by Tom Bamford, is seen powering around a tough turn at the temporary desert race track in Palm Springs, California. A combination of European and American technologies, set in the scenic beauty of Southern California, supported by the glamour of Hollywood but still the domain of the hardcore driver. Although greatly changed from the glory days of the 1950s and 1960s, racing continues at tracks like Laguna Seca and Willow Springs. As the inevitable shift from internal combustion engines to electric motors continues to affect automotive trends in general, so it will affect motorsports. The scene is in for a whole new and exciting era in the sport of racing. (Courtesy of Joel Driskill.)